FIRST 50 SONGS

YOU SHOULD PLAY ON THE MARIMBA

Arrangements by Will Rapp

ISBN 978-1-5400-5457-9

HAL•LEONARD®

Visit Hal Leonard Online at
www.halleonard.com

Contact us:
Hal Leonard
7777 West Bluemound Road
Milwaukee, WI 53213
Email: info@halleonard.com

In Europe, contact:
Hal Leonard Europe Limited
42 Wigmore Street
Marylebone, London, W1U 2RN
Email: info@halleonardeurope.com

In Australia, contact:
Hal Leonard Australia Pty. Ltd.
4 Lentara Court
Cheltenham, Victoria, 3192 Australia
Email: info@halleonard.com.au

CONTENTS

AMAZING GRACE

MARIMBA

Traditional American Melody

BOHEMIAN RHAPSODY

MARIMBA

Words and Music by
FREDDIE MERCURY

Swing ($\sqcap$ = $\sqcap^3\!\flat$)

($\bullet$=$\flat$) **Slowly**
(Straight Eighths)

rit.

BABY ELEPHANT WALK

From the Paramount Picture HATARI!

MARIMBA

By HENRY MANCINI

Light Rock

rit.

CHOUCOUNE
(YELLOW BIRD)

MARIMBA

Haitian Folksong

CIRCLE OF LIFE/NANTS' INGONYAMA
from THE LION KING

MARIMBA

NANTS' INGONYAMA
Music and Lyrics by LEBOHANG MORAKE
and HANS ZIMMER

Moderately (with an African beat)

CIRCLE OF LIFE
Music by ELTON JOHN
Lyrics by TIM RICE

CLOCKS

MARIMBA

Words and Music by GUY BERRYMAN, JON BUCKLAND,
WILL CHAMPION and CHRIS MARTIN

CUMANA

MARIMBA

Words by HAROLD SPINA and ROC HILLMAN
Music by BARCLAY ALLEN

Fast Mambo

CZARDAS

MARIMBA

Traditional Hungarian Folk Dance

DANSE BOHÈME
From CARMEN

MARIMBA

By GEORGES BIZET

DAY-O
(The Banana Boat Song)

MARIMBA

Words and Music by IRVING BURGIE
and WILLIAM ATTAWAY

ETERNAL FATHER, STRONG TO SAVE

MARIMBA

By JOHN BACCHUS DYKES

DON'T YOU WORRY 'BOUT A THING

MARIMBA

Words and Music by
STEVIE WONDER

HAKUNA MATATA
From THE LION KING

MARIMBA

Music by ELTON JOHN
Lyrics by TIM RICE

HELLO, DOLLY!

from HELLO, DOLLY!

MARIMBA

Music and Lyric by
JERRY HERMAN

MARY ANN

MARIMBA

Words and Music by
RAFAEL DE LEON

Calypso

HEY JUDE

MARIMBA

Words and Music by
JOHN LENNON and PAUL McCARTNEY

rit.

HURRICANE SEASON

MARIMBA

By TROY ANDREWS

New Orleans Funk

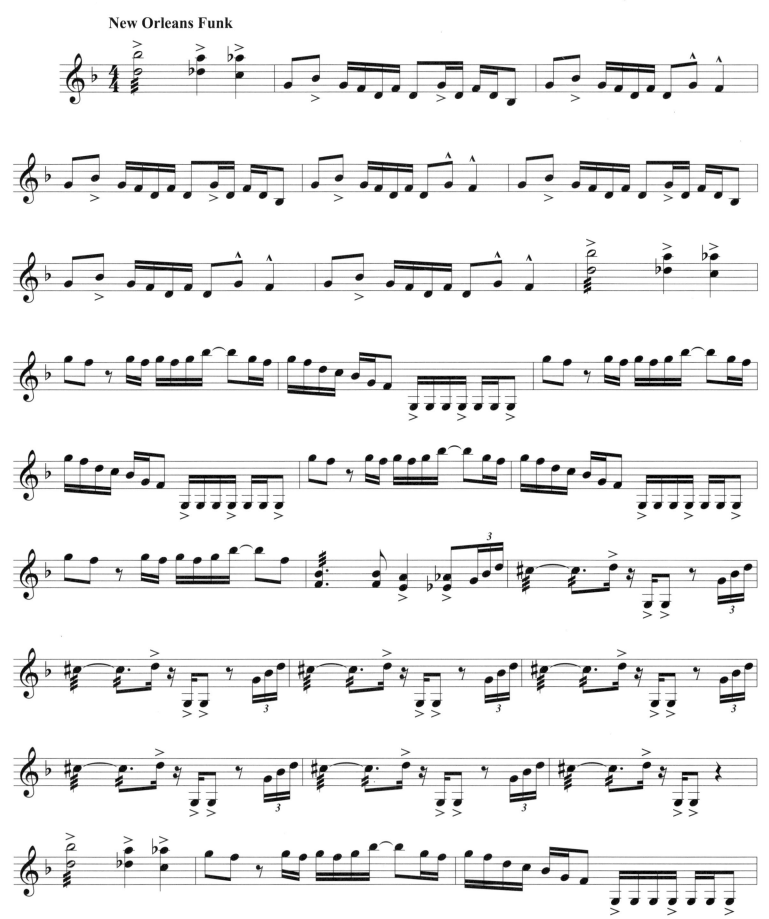

IN THE STONE

MARIMBA

Words and Music by MAURICE WHITE,
DAVID FOSTER and ALLEE WILLIS

JAMAICA FAREWELL

MARIMBA

Words and Music by
IRVING BURGIE

LET IT GO
From FROZEN

MARIMBA

Music and Lyrics by KRISTEN ANDERSON-LOPEZ
and ROBERT LOPEZ

LIMBO ROCK

MARIMBA

Words and Music by BILLY STRANGE
and JON SHELDON

LINUS AND LUCY
from A CHARLIE BROWN CHRISTMAS

MARIMBA

By VINCE GUARALDI

LIVING FOR THE CITY

MARIMBA

Words and Music by
STEVIE WONDER

MAMBO NO. 5
(A Little Bit Of...)

MARIMBA

Original Music by DAMASO PEREZ PRADO
Words by LOU BEGA and ZIPPY

45

MAS QUE NADA

MARIMBA

Words and Music by
JORGE BEN

MICHELLE

MARIMBA

Words and Music by JOHN LENNON
and PAUL McCARTNEY

MY FAVORITE THINGS

from THE SOUND OF MUSIC

MARIMBA

Lyrics by OSCAR HAMMERSTEIN II
Music by RICHARD RODGERS

OLD JOE CLARK

MARIMBA

Tennessee Folksong

ON BROADWAY

MARIMBA

Words and Music by BARRY MANN, CYNTHIA WEIL,
MIKE STOLLER and JERRY LEIBER

ONE NOTE SAMBA
(Samba De Uma Nota So)

MARIMBA

Original Lyrics by NEWTON MENDONÇA
English Lyrics by ANTONIO CARLOS JOBIM
Music by ANTONIO CARLOS JOBIM

Bright Samba

PETER GUNN
Theme Song from the Television Series

MARIMBA

By HENRY MANCINI

OYE COMO VA

MARIMBA

Words and Music by
TITO PUENTE

57

+ = Dead Stroke

PERFIDIA

MARIMBA

Words and Music by
ALBERTO DOMINGUEZ

PIRATES OF THE CARIBBEAN
from PIRATES OF THE CARIBBEAN: THE CURSE OF THE BLACK PEARL

MARIMBA

THE MEDALLION CALLS
Music by KLAUS BADELT
Majestically

TO THE PIRATE'S CAVE!
Music by KLAUS BADELT
Driving!

THE BLACK PEARL
Music by KLAUS BADELT

Faster

PROUD MARY

MARIMBA

Words and Music by
JOHN FOGERTY

QUIET NIGHTS OF QUIET STARS
(Corcovado)

MARIMBA

Original Words and Musioc by
ANTONIO CARLOS JOBIM

THE SHADOW OF YOUR SMILE
Love Theme from THE SANDPIPER

MARIMBA

Music by JOHNNY MANDEL
Words by PAUL FRANCIS WEBSTER

SO THIS IS LOVE
from CINDERELLA

MARIMBA

Words and Music by AL HOFFMAN,
MACK DAVID and JERRY LIVINGSTON

Tenderly

SHALLOW

from A STAR IS BORN

Words and Music by STEFANI GERMANOTTA,
MARK RONSON, ANDREW WYATT and ANTHONY ROSSOMANDO

Marimba

SO WHAT

MARIMBA

By MILES DAVIS

rit.

THE STAR-SPANGLED BANNER

MARIMBA

Words by FRANCIS SCOTT KEY
Music by JOHN STAFFORD SMITH

TANGERINE

MARIMBA

Words by JOHNNY MERCER
Music by VICTOR SCHERTZINGER

WAVE

MARIMBA

Words and Music by
ANTONIO CARLOS JOBIM

Bossa Nova

VIVA LA VIDA

MARIMBA

Words and Music by GUY BERRYMAN,
JON BUCKLAND, WILL CHAMPION and CHRIS MARTIN

TEQUILA

MARIMBA

By CHUCK RIO

UNDER THE SEA
from THE LITTLE MERMAID

MARIMBA

Music by ALAN MENKIN
Lyrics by HOWARD ASHMAN

WE WILL ROCK YOU

MARIMBA

Words and Music by
BRIAN MAY

YESTERDAY

MARIMBA

Words and Music by JOHN LENNON
and PAUL McCARTNEY

WIPE OUT

MARIMBA

By THE SURFARIS

Surf Rock

YES! WE HAVE NO BANANAS

MARIMBA

By FRANK SILVER and IRVING COHN

     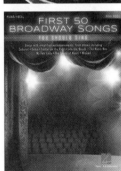
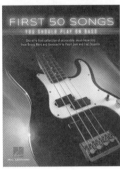